If the caption fits...

THE BEST OF THE PUNCH CAPTION COMPETITION

First published in Great Britain 1981
by Elm Tree Books/Hamish Hamilton Ltd
Garden House 57–59 Long Acre London WC2E 9JZ

Book design by Glyn Rees

British Library Cataloguing in Publication Data
If the caption fits
   1. English wit and humor, Pictorial
   I. Sale, Jonathan
   II. Punch
   741.5′942   NC1476
   ISBN 0–241–10668–0

Printed and bound in Great Britain by
Richard Clay (The Chaucer Press) Ltd, Bungay, Suffolk

If the caption fits...

THE BEST OF THE PUNCH CAPTION COMPETITION

Edited by Jonathan Sale

ELM TREE BOOKS

LONDON

Judging it

Sometimes, as we open the envelopes, we begin to think there ought to be some sort of intelligence test for readers of *Punch*. Why, when presented with a Victorian cartoon of a vicar playing marbles upside down in a lion's cage, cannot they come up with a brand new caption that takes account of all those elements and is still wry and topical? Perhaps we should make sure that *Punch* falls only into the hands of those with certain standards of humour, observation, general knowledge and awareness of current affairs — who combine all that with the possession of a first-class stamp and the ability to find a letter-box in time to allow delivery by first post on Tuesday after the issue appears.

Perhaps, the more we think about it, the Caption Competition is more difficult than it seems. It is hard enough for a cartoonist to come up with a brand-new gag even when he has the freedom to alter his drawing to fit the words he plans to put underneath it.

What we ask readers to do, every week, is to look at a couple of cartoons lifted from dusty back-numbers and add a caption that breathes life into the aged lines. The drawing, of course, is unalterable. No good wishing that a different character was speaking or that one man looked more like Cyril Smith and another less like Danny La Rue.

We select the two best captions and print them, this time with the originals, which first saw the light of day anything from fifty to one hundred years ago. The amusing thing about the original lines, is, in many cases,

that anyone thought them amusing all those years ago. They go on for ever, some of the original captions, with two or more speakers, like a short play whose curtain-line is that the servant's command of French isn't what it might be or that a nouveau riche chappie is liable to fall off his horse. Did none of the public in the 1870s beat on the editor's door and demand their money back? Certainly our readers today bring a sharper gag than our artists then. (Very occasionally the two coincide. We once set a picture of a man in a trance, his face suffused with a beatific smile, while behind him stood a character with his hand raised. "This," suggested a reader, "is how to strike a happy medium." So, alas, did the original caption, so the prize — oh yes, there is money involved — went to someone else. I'm not saying that there was any cheating or cribbing, but one can't be too careful.)

What does often get the prize is a line which pokes fun at the drawing, either by juxtaposing a cheeky phrase to a stately illustration, or by pointing out the artist's technical shortcomings. Where a cartoonist has economised on ink while drawing a character's leg, an alert reader will offer something about a stolen kneecap. Where a tug-of-war rope is ambiguously sketched, a reader will suggest it looks more like a public dis-embowelling. Not for nothing do we have a policy of using the work of artists who are very dead.

What has got the prize, but won't again, is any caption that, accompanying any character who is vaguely out of the ordinary like a tramp or middle-aged nurse, goes something like, "No, it's me, Watson," or even, "Elementary" etc etc. We have had a lot of computer dating over the last ten years, but never, save in exceptional circumstances, again. You can use the joke about a turn-of-the-century matron being really a fellow in drag only so many times. A rather stiffly executed policeman may prompt the thought that he is really a statue or large wind-up doll once, but just the once. Do not, faced with a drawing in which someone has raised his right foot a fraction of an inch from the ground, tell us that "You do the Hokey-Cokey." Back in the early Seventies, we liked that one, but it doesn't wear well over the years.

In making a selection from more than a decade of Competitions, many winners have been pruned. Too much topicality makes a joke incomprehensible. Did Elton John have a hair transplant? Or Frank Sinatra? Who was the dead Bulgarian, and was an umbrella really the weapon? As for George Davis, was he Innocent or not? You would need footnotes. Doubtless some American professors are poised to leap upon this volume as the basis for a thesis on Changing Psychology in an On-going Humor Situation, or Laughter Motivation in English Perspective. And very well they will do it, too. They won't win any Caption Competitions, though.

Jonathan Sale

Doing it

When our Caption Competition clocked up its 500th test of readers' wits, regular contester C. THOMSON OF GLASGOW described his weekly struggle . . .

Wake up. Wednesday. *Punch* Caption Competition Day! Fall asleep.

Once more the struggle to thrash out an immortal line, to out-Groucho Groucho, to roll Wodehouse, Thurber, Milligan and Shuttleworth into a single sentence. Shuttleworth? I was at school with Shuttleworth. Funniest bloke I ever met. He had that happy schoolboy knack of honing the very nub of any situation into a few scalpel-sharp words and actions, carving the human tragedy along a clearer line, setting acutely observed elements one against the other, achieving an effect both original yet achingly familiar. More important, he had a funny name like Shuttleworth.

No sidetracking! Buy that mag! Scan that cartoon! Write that immortal line! Make the readership rock with raucous laughter, make eager entrants give grudging grins.

Can't be bothered.

I buy a *Punch*. Flip open back page. Bend down. Am not doubled up in merriment. Am recovering leaflet ad for luxurious watermarked laid writing paper, embossed for me, with matching envelopes and correspondence cards. Throw ad in pavement litter bin. Throw self at opposite pavement as Scottish & Newcastle juggernaut swoops at me out of malice and sun. Flip open back page. Yes, haven't won it again!

I confess. I do it every week. The Caption Competition. It's on the second-last back page, probably facing a full-colour ad for twelve-year-old malt. Remind me to work in a gag about going against the grain. That competition is an obsession. Addiction.

Craze. Mania. Habit. Albatross.

The Ancient Mariner would sympathise with my self-inflicted task. If he had any sympathy for anyone other than himself, that is. Probably too busy writing repentant letters to the RSPB. With an albatross quill. And that Greek chap (his name, now, was it Polydopoulous?), the one with the vultures pecking his living flesh every day. He'd understand. Remind me to work in a gag about luncheon vultures. Oh, eagles, was it? Pardon me.

Perhaps it's something to do with self-flagellation, this weekly discipline. Good for the soul, especially if your soul is a Knox-Calvin-Luther-Scots-angst-ridden one like mine.

Bet John Knox wouldn't approve of Caption Competitions. You'd be lashed to a stake before you could say "Protestant work ethic". There you'd be — codpiece-deep in dry kindling, flames dancing around you, your literary licence revoked. "Thank goodness it's only a first offence," you'd be saying.

The Moderator of the General Assembly isn't going to like this kind of talk. Some of you may not know who The Moderator is. He is neither a character from *Doctor Who* nor a militant shop steward from Dagenham. He's far more frightening.

Definitely can't be bothered this week. Too frightened.

Flip open back page. Same old routine. How about a pun this time? Intensive research in *Punch* archives under bed reveals only two winning puns in last year. That makes starting price on Puns about 50/1 . . . Politics (blinkered runner) 20/1 . . . Topicality 3/1 . . . Miscellaneous, evens favourite. Topicality presents good each way gamble on getting surname and first initial into *Punch*. Quick hunt through today's paper should pay dividends.

Let's see that paper. Violence . . . corruption . . . brutality . . . glamour . . . high finance . . . greed . . . latest hair styles. So much for the sports pages.

Why not simply plump for the favourite, Miscellaneous? It's easy. Just link the competition cartoon with something from your everyday life. Say, for instance, you are the leader of a fanatical Islamic nostalgia boom. Maybe this week's cartoon links with something both Islamic and nostalgic — like amputation.

Yes, it's invaluable to have a firm grip of general knowledge and current affairs. Blue salt bags did the trick the other week. The price of sprouts, secret ballots, the Shavian Society, Lord Lucan, Greek tankers, Bulgarian umbrellas. Every one a winner.

Eclectics. That's the secret. It takes a lot of energy to be eclectic. Remind me to work in gag about eclecticity generators. The Eclectics: official political wing of Spanish Inquisition Rack Maintenance Engineers. Disbanded 1563 after referendum revealed less than 40% of population knew what "eclectic" meant.

Eclectics: exciting kid's game, with battery-operated racing cars and easy-assemble plastic track.

Eclectics: system of collective economics first developed by Danish Agriculture Ministry in the early 1960s.

Now I really can't be bothered. Hold on while I look up "eclectics".

Look, about this Caption Competition. If you do want to enter, don't, on any account, whatever you do, don't — it won't get you anywhere — do not be direct. Allude. Infer. Imply. Hint. Tip the wink. Insinuate. Look out a Thesaurus. That's my final solution if I'm stuck. Roget, over and out.

Let's do an example. Show all your working and do the final answer in ink on a fresh page. Remember to number the question. You have 24 hours. Go!

That's another thing. *Punch* comes out in London on a Tuesday, I've discovered. It only arrives in Glasgow Central Station on Wednesday morning, National Union of Sleeper Creosoters permitting. If entries must be in by first post Monday . . . mine go second class, being a bawbee-scrimping, tightfisted, canny Scot with all my brains in my feet for the football, that means post at the very latest first thing Friday! Only Wednesday and Thursday to think about your caption — instant disadvantage. Is it any wonder the Scots are the world's best-balanced personalities, with a chip on both shoulders?

Not me, of course. Not enough room for two chips *and* an albatross.

And that's why nobody from Shetland ever wins the Caption Competition. I mean, for all we know, K. Rasmussen of Virkie is a genius with a penned wit like harnessed thunder, but his postcards only reach the *Punch* in-tray by second post July. With a frank-mark over the caption.

Where was I? Ah, yes, the example. Take a typical cartoon from 1875. Immaculately drawn, very dark, Victorian boxwood print. Top-hatted gent mounted back to front on a galloping stallion, blowing a hunting horn. Picnic party scatters before him, crinolines aflap. English wooded landscape.

. . . your mind's a blank, eh? So's mine and I am the person who actually thought up the example.

Think laterally. Even better, think sideways. To the drawer over there where the Gypsy Creams are. No, no, keep at it! Think what goes with horses. Gypsy Creams. No, no, Belgians go with horses. In fact, Belgians go pretty well all the way with horses. Boiled, scrambled, poached — mostly poached from Britain.

No, the Belgian angle won't do. We're in the EEC now. Wogs don't begin at Calais any more. They usually begin in Marks & Spencer, saying "Zut, regardez ce all-wool knitwearl" and snapping up our bargain, cut-rate shoplifting fines — "Name of a pipe, trois twin sets ce n'est qu'un severe ticking off, VAT inclusif."

Okay, forget horses. Try combining picnics with blood-sports.

Tricky, isn't it? Yet mine is a standard enough example. Someone, somewhere, browses through endless back numbers of *Punch*, poring over old captions, each lovingly crafted to well over 20 words, with explicit instructions on how to understand the joke. I love them. The old captions, not the browsers. My concentration's gone.

Can't be bothered at all with this week's entry. The hell with it. Wander to window. Stare blankly at rear of Scottish & Amicable building. I'm Scottish and amicable and if you don't agree I'll break your nose. Gypsy Creams all gone. Coffee cold. Hands in pockets. Rattle change.

A squad of crack *Punch* quipsters must be down there in EC4, drumming their fingers on the chequebook, itching to bang off two whole tenners across the nation. Sumptious ackers. Lolly. Filthy lucre. Bugs Bunny. Cadbury's Smash. The Root of All Evil.

Now I'm bothered.

C. Thomson of Glasgow

POSTSCRIPT
Not long after this article appeared in *Punch,* a blank Competition entry form arrived. It bore a Glasgow postmark and it was from C. Thomson. Under his name, he had written, "I give up." We have never heard from him since.

The winners

JOINT WINNERS: "*Do you suppose that they ever suspect we're from the Michelin Guide?*"

AND: "*Moonshot 2 to Mission Control—we're running late again.*"

C. Hollingworth of Bangor.

1876 caption.—PATENT FIRST-CLASS COSTUME FOR THE COLLISION SEASON. Traveller. "*Yes, it's decidedly Warm, but there's a feeling of Security about it I rather like.*" (Yawns.) "*Any Chance of a Smash to-Day!?*" (Drops off to Sleep!)

"*I believe they both work at the Weather Centre.*"

C. Marris of London W2.

1928 caption.—ENTERTAINMENTS AT WHICH WE HAVE NEVER ASSISTED. The Gardener's Wedding.

"*Mr. Constable's changed his mind—get the hay off it again.*"

K. S. Gay of Bury St. Edmunds, Suffolk

1901 caption—Giles: "I be got up here, Mister, but I don't zee 'ow ever I be goin' to get down."
Farmer: "Thee zhut thee eyes an' walk about a bit, an' thee'll zoon get down!"

"*Time for your paper round, m'Lord.*"

M. Birch of Grays, Essex.

1939 caption.—"*Anything special on the crisis page, Ellis?*"

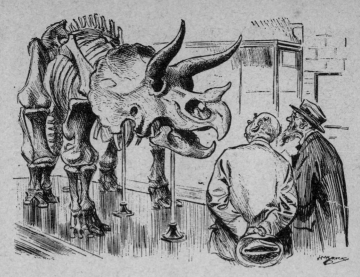

"Arthritis wiped them out overnight."

W. Shackleton of Rutherglen, Lanarkshire

1927 caption—"This animal was called the Triceratops Prorsus."
"Not to its face I presume."

*"All right, that'll do. You lads know the rules of the prisoners'
drama group as well as I do."*

J. Oldacre of Brixham, Devon

1917 caption—Voice from gallery (during grave-digger scene in 'Hamlet'): *"Ain't yer
going to 'ave no parapet?"*

"Pawn to Queen Two. . . ."

I. Rowbotham of Manchester.

1879 caption—INFORMAL INTRODUCTIONS. Apple-Coster: *"Here you are, gents! All four of 'em sweet and fresh as can be!"*

"Course, it'll be better when we've got the curtains up."

G. Vincent of London, SW5

1927 caption—The One: *"Why not greyhound racing?"*
The Other: *"That's an idea."*

"Who do we know in Rome?"

M. Keen of Brighton

1950 caption.—"Henry's considering a compromise on the vesting date for the monasteries."

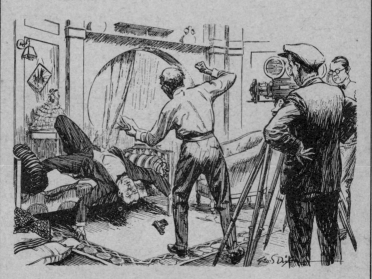

"Some people get so dramatic for a passport photo."

A. Katz of London, N.3.

1924 caption—*"No. No. No! That's not the way to die! Put more life into it."*

"I call it 'Birds In Flight'."

J. Tulip of Ewell, Surrey.

1931 caption—Plumber (with dignity, as the lady of the house interrupts his work): *"Afore you speaks, Mum, I'll tell you I knows all the jokes concerning my perfession. I've got all me tools 'ere—I remains till I've located the leakage—I ain't going back for nothin' and I ain't got no mate."* Lady: *"But there's nothing the matter here. You've come to the wrong house."*

"You must agree that MI5 really knows how to give an annual dinner."

W. Halliday of Belfast.

1925 caption.—ENTERTAINMENTS AT WHICH WE HAVE NEVER ASSISTED. A Dinner at the Thespian Club.

"*Now that he's gone, Your Majesty, it could keep your mind off things.*"

T. M. Callaghan of Darlington

1913 caption—CHRISTMAS PRESENTS: Customer: "*All these seem very expensive: can't you suggest something cheaper?*"

Shopman (with views on commercial morality): "*Certainly, madam, I could suggest a piece of thin paper and a comb.*"

"*Now the other pocket . . .*"

A. Tatton-Brawn of Bath, Somerset

1934 caption.—The Motorist buys his son a Christmas present of an Educational Nature.

"Say what you like about King Kong, he's a tidy eater."

J. Hardy of London, EC1

1933 caption.—*"Lumme, Joe! I s'pose that was the 'ouse?"*

"You're the heaviest, you answer the door."

C. H. Johnson of Congleton, Cheshire

1860 caption.—A RISE IN BREAD-STUFFS—EFFECTS OF EATING AERATED BREAD: Poor Cocker having been Recommended to try the "Aerated Bread," does so, and is Discovered, along with his Family, Floating about the Ceiling of his Parlour, in an utterly Helpless Condition.

"So much for the long-range weather forecast!"

D. E. Pickstock of Belfast, N.I.

1938 caption.—*"To bring about this result, I shall explore every seal-hole and leave no iceberg unturned."*

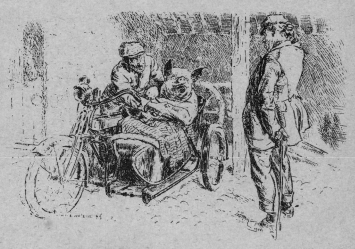

"Why can't you just bring sandwiches, like everyone else!"

B. M. Heath of London S.E.13.

1918 caption—THE LADY WHO PAYS THE RENT. *"Glory be, Pat, but what are ye doin' with the pig?"* *"Giving the cratur a bit of divarshun. Sure with the price she'll be fetchin' me, how could I be dhrivin' her in the ass's cart?"*

"*I wish he'd tell me when he's going to bring his drinking pals back for lunch.*"

R. C. Wallis of Wembley, Middx.

1949 caption.—"*Don't look, dear—here come those dreadful Argonauts.*"

"*I'm afraid I shall have to fail you on your three-point turn, madam.*"

G. Tyler of Braintree, Essex

1927 caption.—*Overwrought wife:* "*Don't stand there like an idiot! I thought you always got underneath to see what's the matter.*"

"Now that you've caught it, what are you going to do with it?"

A. Vaughan Rees of Swansea, S. Wales

1926 caption.—Modernist (discussing the Academy): *"Well, they've chucked all my things—but they shan't cow me into doing understandable stuff."*

"Hear those drums, brigadier? It means there's a rock festival in the village."

L. P. Rowley of Leeds

1929 caption.—Scientist (to Old Lady): *"There are twenty million stars in the heavens."* Old Lady (brightly) *"So I see."*

"Have you been waiting long?"

D. Williams of Brighton, Sussex.

1933 caption.—Husband (shipwrecked on desert island, to wife): *"Well, my dear, without being in any way unpatriotic, we* are *escaping from an English spring!"*

"Are you sure he's drowning?"

R. C. L. Hunter of Chesham, Bucks.

1927 caption.—The Woman (to unenterprising swain): *"I think that unlighted cigarette just suits you."*

"Wanna buy a pince-nez, lady?"

D. A. Stocks of London, W.1.

1936 caption.—*"What an ideal position for mountains, Jane."*

"And the only thing stolen was your right knee-cap?"

H. O'Donnell of London, N.15

1940 caption.—*"Now I would like to organise the whole world . . ."*

Joint Winners: "*Gimme the moonlight . . .*"

L. Roden of Woodford Green, Essex

"*I'm afraid I've trodden on your daughter's stick insect.*"

N. Craig of London E11

1921 caption.—Village Idiot. "*Beg yer pardon, Mum—seein' as ye was paintin' the church I thought I'd better tell ye the clock be ten minutes fast.*"

"*Take it back, it's only firing on two.*"

A. Churchley of Plymouth.

1927 caption.—Early adaption of local monster.

"OK—put the case with the cash in over the rail, and I'll regurgitate your husband."

C. Vanlint of Chelmsford, Essex

1939 caption—"ANYONE WOULDN'T THINK THEY WAS 'ARDLY HUMAN."

"Another first, Mr Bonnington—the South face of Everest in drag."

T. Wood of Brighton, Sussex

1900 caption—*HOSTESS.* "WHAT DO YOU THINK OF OUR GAME PIE, MR BRIGSON? WE RATHER PRIDE OURSELVES ON IT, YOU KNOW." *BRIGSON (NERVOUSLY ANXIOUS TO PLEASE).* "OH, THANK YOU, IT'S VERY NICE INDEED, WHAT THERE IS OF IT. WHAT I MEAN TO SAY IS, THERE'S PLENTY OF IT—SUCH AS IT IS!" [Awful pause.]

"It's the way you tell them, Mrs Whitehouse."
M. J. Smallcombe of Claygate.

1938 caption—"OH DO GO ON TELLING US ABOUT DEPORTMENT."

"I didn't know Pamplona were t'bloody twin town."
M. Holt of Walsall

1900 caption—**CREAM OF TARTAR.** ["AT THE EASTERN COUNTIES DAIRY FARMER'S DINNER THE OTHER DAY, HE (PROFESSOR McCONNEL) STATED THAT MUSIC, SUITABLE IN QUALITY, AND ADMINISTERED AT THE RIGHT MOMENT, WAS A NEVER-FAILING MEANS OF INCREASING THE SUPPLY OF CREAM."—*DAILY PAPER*]

*"OK, so they got the first goal, but we have another
15 minutes in which to equalise."*

C. Jonklaas of Watford.

1876 caption.—SOCIAL BEINGS. Wearied by London Dissipation, the Marjoribanks
Browns go, for the sake of perfect Quiet, to that Picturesque little Watering-Place,
Shrimpington-super-Mare, where they trust that they will not meet a single Soul they
know. Oddly enough, the Cholmondeley Jones go to the same Spot with the same
Purpose. Now, these Jones and Browns cordially detest each other in London, and
and are not even on speaking Terms; yet, such is the depressing effect of "perfect
Quiet" that, as soon as they meet in Shrimpington-super-Mare, they rush into each
other's Arms with a wild Sense of Relief!

"It's all right—our MP's in favour of cheese coursing."

P. Haywood of Liversedge, Yorkshire.

1928 caption.—ENTERTAINMENTS AT WHICH WE HAVE NEVER ASSISTED.
Quaint survival of an ancient custom in an old-world village near Cheddar—
"Welshing the Rabbit."

JOINT WINNERS: *"And at that point, gentlemen, the encyclopedia is as good as sold."*

A. Mitchell of Woldingham

AND   *"Rubbish! It's nothing like Notre Dame."*

C. Thomson of Glasgow

1931 caption—ENTERTAINMENTS AT WHICH WE HAVE NEVER ASSISTED."BALANCING THE BOOKS" AT THE ANNUAL DINNER OF THE SOCIETY OF CHARTERED ACCOUNTANTS..

"I think Thor Heyerdahl's definitely got this one wrong."

M. Green of Kew

1931 caption—METEOROLOGICAL OFFICE ACTIVITIES. STAVING OFF A COLD SNAP ON THE CORNISH COAST.

"*Don't move. He's gone to get his rubber.*"

J. Peebles of Boston, Lincolnshire

1937 caption.—"*Well, what can you do?*" "*Haven't you noticed?*"

"*Roll up! Knock me in the water and win a lantern.*"

B. Black of Bedford.

1937 caption.—"*He inherited it from his ancestors, and the Foo-Choo Harbour Company have now practically given up all hope of ever buying him out.*"

"Now, for the last time—which one of you is going to write Wuthering Heights?"

C. M. Gill of London SW13.

1881 caption.—REMOVAL OF ANCIENT LANDMARKS. *Lady Gwendoline.* "Papa says *I'm* to be a Great Artist, and exhibit at the Royal Academy!" *Lady Yseulte.* "And Papa says *I'm* to be a great Pianist, and play at the Monday Pops!" *Lady Edelgitha.* "And I'm going to be a famous Actress, and act *Ophelia*, and cut out Miss Ellen Terry! Papa says I may—that is, if I *can*, you know!" *The New Governess.* "Goodness gracious, Young Ladies! Is it possible His Grace can allow you even to *think* of such things! Why, my Papa was only a poor Half-pay Officer, but the bare thought of my ever playing in *public*, or painting for *hire*, would have simply horrified him!—and as for acting Ophelia—or anything else—gracious goodness you take my breath away!"

*"Yes, it beheads them **and** prints the obituaries."*

P. C. Fitton of Rochdale, Lancs.

1928 caption.—OLD ENGLISH CUSTOMS. Inhabitants of Great Smugglebury performing the annual ceremony of mangling the wurzel.

"Personally, I don't think it was a ticket collector in the other carriage."

I. Harris of London W4

1937 caption.—*"Oh yes, I'd always give up my seat to a lady—if one ever succeeded in fighting her way in."*

"Why don't they carry a transistor, like everyone else?"

A. Cole of Shoreham, Kent

1862 caption.—*A sea-side subject:— Jolly for the party in search of repose. N.B. The Old Lady with the Parrot encourages Organ-Grinders, and when the Moon shines bright and clear, doesn't the Black Dog come out!*

"I've just had a wonderful idea for an everyday story of country folk."

J. Duthoit of Scarborough

1862 caption.—Practising for a match. Leonora. "*Dear! Dear! How the arrow sticks!*" Capt. Blank (with a sigh of the deepest). "*It does, indeed!*"

"I can't see the croupier accepting that—there's a complete Rolls already on the Black Seven."

J. Hughes of St. Helier, Jersey

1930 caption.—Safety first. How to defeat the motor-thieves when parking your car.

JOINT WINNERS: *"All right—which one of you lot pinched the ham out of my sandwich?"*

R. Morris of Chesterfield

AND: *"Bad news from the front, Sassoon—the Hun's perfected a rhyming dictionary."*

P. Fitton of Rochdale

1877 caption—GARRISON INSTRUCTION. *INSTRUCTOR (LECTURING).* "GENTLEMEN, A THREE-LEGGED TRESTLE IS A TRESTLE WITH THREE LEGS. YOU HAD BETTER MAKE A NOTE OF THAT, GENTLEMEN." *(INTENSE SCRIBBLING.) GENERAL IN EMBRYO (BUT NOT AT PRESENT NOTED FOR SMARTNESS),* AFTER A PAUSE OF SOME MINUTES. "I BEG YOUR PARDON, MAJOR, BUT HOW MANY LEGS DID YOU SAY THE TRESTLE HAD?" *(LEFT SITTING.)*

"Now that fuel's scarce, most wives seem to be running their husbands to the station."

T. Wood of Brighton.

1938 caption—"WE'RE LEADING NOW, YOUR GRACE!"

*"Right, we've seen the film. We must now ask ourselves
what effect it is likely to have on ordinary people."*

T. Newton of York

1862 caption.—A SPIRIT RAPPING SEANCE. Mr. Foxer (a medium): "*Oh dear! There's a
spirit named Walker writing on my arm!*"

*"I wonder if the world is **really** waiting for the
oven-ready hedgehog . . ."*

Sally Bateman of London W11

1930 caption.—Preparation for the Horticultural Show. A competitor putting belladona
in the eyes of his potatoes.

JOINT WINNERS: "*I said, 'That's £4,962.43 on the meter from Charing Cross,' Guv.*"   J. Hicks of Oxford

"*And I say it's bedtime.*"   V. Mackenzie of St. Albans

1930 caption.—STUDIES IN CRIME. Kidnapping the heir to the throne of Toshkistan.

"*Well, just a half. I can see I shall have to carry my sister home.*"

J. L. Woods of Weymouth, Dorset

1862 caption.—Elder Sister. "*Gus, there's your Cousin Rosa sitting down. Why don't you ask her to dance?*" Augustus. "*Well, I've danced with her twice already, you know; and people are so disagreeable, if I trotted her out again, they'd be sure to talk about it!*"

"Give me a hand will ye, it's his birthday."

C. Murphy of York

1860 caption.—MR. BRIGGS IN THE HIGHLANDS. Mr. Briggs, previous to going through his course of Deer-Stalking, assists the Forester in getting a Hart or two for the House. Donald is requesting our Friend to hold the Animal down by its Horns. (N.B. the Said Animal is as strong as a Bull, and uses his legs like a Race-horse.)

"There's no future in these Agincourt reunions, you know."

G. Buchanan of Witney, Oxon.

1930 caption.—Exclusive Person (entering dining-room of his club). *"Dammit! Where the doose can I go? There's somebody got my table."*

"I think it's about time the National Front learnt to organise a rally!"

F. Marshal of Camberley

1934 caption—UNFORTUNATE POSITION OF SKATER WHEN ONLY PASSER-BY WAS A FASCIST.

"Mum says thanks but Dad's dead and is there anything back on this?"

T. Laurence of London W11

1910 caption—LITTLE GIRL. "PLEASE, SIR, I'VE BROUGHT THE REMAINS OF THE MEDICINE YOU GAVE GRANDFATHER. HE'S DEAD, AND MOTHER THOUGHT YOU MIGHT LIKE IT FOR SOMEBODY ELSE!"

"Mention a new motorway and the pedestrian lobby will always over-react."

A. Pantin of Harrogate

1936 caption—"IF YOU WILL KINDLY TAKE A SEAT, SIR JOSHUA WON'T KEEP YOU A MOMENT. THIS IS THE LAST EXERCISE."

"She was talking to the plant, officer, and it swore at her."

A. Walker of Rottingdean

1931 caption—UNDER A MINISTRY OF PUBLIC TASTE. POLICE RAIDING A HOUSE FOR CONCEALED ASPIDISTRAS.

"I name this ship . . . hang on a minute!"

D. Holman of Berkhamsted, Herts.

1929 caption.—Holiday reactions. Absconding treasurer of a Share-out Club
endeavouring to avoid arrest.

"Mine's not bad—but I don't think much of yours!"

E. Runham of Chigwell, Essex

1888 caption.—WHAT OUR ARTIST HAS TO PUT UP WITH.—(The Anti-Beauty
Crusade in Modern Art Criticism.) Eminent Art Critic. "Yes, my young Friend—as
I have often said in Print—you, in common with all the Modern English School of
Female Figure Painters, are depraved by a morbid and inane love of *Prettiness*, to the
exclusion of all the sterner qualities of *Character, Reality, Truth to Nature* —A—A—
by the way, here come my Wife and Daughters, who share my Views. Let me intro-
duce you." (Our Artist understands the Eminent Critic's point of view, and forgives
him.)

"And now, to follow Mr. Price's very successful bird imitations . . ."

M. Wirt of London SE21.

1889 caption.—HAPPY THOUGHT. The Electric Light, so favourable to Furniture, Wall Papers, Pictures, Screens, &c., is not always becoming to the Female Complexion. Light Japanese Sunshades will be found invaluable.

JOINT WINNERS. *"Now will you join the Musicians' Union?"*

S. Davies of Wirral, Cheshire.

and *"I wish you'd put it in my mouth. I can't suck it up quickly enough."*

D. Spittal of Argyll.

1930 caption.—PIONEERS OF MUSIC. The inventor of a deadly type of wind-instrument suffers the penalty of his crime.

" *You should have gone before we started.*"

J. Salmon of Loughton, Essex.

1890 caption.—"THE YOUNG PEOPLE'S ORCHESTRAL CONCERT." ALL INFANT PRODIGIES. Picture of a Rehearsal, by One who wasn't there.

"*We don't mind, because she keeps the mice down.*"

B. Whelan of Farnham, Surrey.

1930 caption.—We may one day find women keeping them in condition on a table-leg.

"Messy stuff, asparagus."

J. Woods of Weymouth, Dorset.

1890 caption.—BARBERESSES.

JOINT WINNERS: *"Quite unprecedented—the whole escort agency's been stood up."*

P. Fitton of Cambridge.

AND: *"The little fellow's the one to watch when the trouble starts."*

J. Fox of Bristol.

1897 caption.—RETRENCHMENT. Jinks. "*Don't meet you 'ere so often as we used to, Binks, eh?*" Binks. "*Well—no. It don't run to a Hopera-Box this Season, because, you see, we've took a Window for this 'ere Jubilee.*"

"I can't move—somebody's nailed my left shoe to the floor."
L. Rowley of Leeds

1927 caption.—MANNERS AND MODES. Study of a wife revenging herself on a husband who has persistently condemned the modern fashions.

"Our Gran wanted it to be dignified without being miserable."

J. Woods of Weymouth, Dorset

1868 caption.—IN JEOPARDY. The new Boy was enjoined to be very careful how he carried the Fiddle-Case—"*By he handle, and to mind not to knock it against anything!*" Imagine the horror of Mr. Pitsey Carter, his master, who was following, to come upon the rascal, with the invaluable "Joseph" on his head, executing a pas seul over a skipping rope!!

"*Is this your **first** exorcism, vicar?*"

J. H. Lewis of Oxford

1927 caption.—Life's little worries: the bedroom bat.

"*Keep him laughing, Dora—if he closes his mouth
I'm done for.*"

R. May of Chigwell, Essex.

1869 caption.—A GENTLE VEGETARIAN. "'*Morning, Miss! Who'd ever think,
looking at us two, that you devoured Bullocks and Sheep, and I never took anything
but Rice?*'"

"I believe it's a random dope test."

J. Rushton of Newport, Salop.

1926 caption.—ENTERTAINMENTS AT WHICH WE HAVE NEVER ASSISTED.
Feeding the ravens at the Tower.

"Bad news, Vicar—Apache markings!"

J. Kent of London N14.

1894 caption.—"THE COURSE OF TRUE LOVE," &c. Scene—Hounds on drag of
Otter, which has turned up small tributary stream. Miss Di (six feet in her stockings,
to deeply-enamoured Curate, five feet three in his, whom she has inveigled out
Otter-hunting). *"Oh, do just Pick me up and Carry me across. It's rather Deep, don't
you know!"* (The Rev. Spooner's sensations are somewhat mixed.)

"This is the last time I agree to coach a 'United Ulster' crew!"

A. Cole of Sevenoaks, Kent.

1869 caption.—NOVEL SCULLING MATCH, in one boat, and on a small pond. *"Now, Girls, whichever Side bumps the Shore first, Wins! So, One, Two, Three, and Away! And, if you like, I will be the Prize!"*

JOINT WINNERS: *"A hundred million quid to get the first barrel ashore and they can't find a can opener."*

P. Plummer of Altrincham, Cheshire.

AND: *"That's no way to auction the Young Pretender's hat-box."*

D. Young of Forgandenny, Perthshire.

1925 caption.—ENTERTAINMENTS AT WHICH WE HAVE NEVER ASSISTED "Banging the Saxpence" at the Caledonian Club.

"*Nice try, but we've moved the barriers.*"

P. Haywood of Leeds.

1925 caption.—BRIGHTER LONDON. SPEEDING UP THE ESCALATOR.

JOINT WINNERS: "*I wish Moss Bros would be more discreet about repossession.*"

P. Fitton of Rochdale

AND: "*I though so, less than 1 m.m. tread and you're nicked.*"

C. Gold of Woodford Green

1937 caption.—COMMON SCENE IN THE CITY. THE DESPATTING OF AN UNFORTUNATE MEMBER OF THE STOCK EXCHANGE ON CONTANGO DAY."

"*An open-air Vera Lynn concert was doomed
from the start.*"

D. Swift of Huddersfield.

1898 caption.—HYDE PARK, MAY 1. Country Cousin. "*What is the meaning of this,
Policeman?*" Constable. "*Labour Day, Miss.*"

"*Yes, the W.C. attendants are still on strike.*"

D. Siddons of Harrow, Middlesex.

1885 caption.—"*OUT IN THE COLD.*"

"I told Cap'n he always takes the Horn too fast."

D. Ellis Williams of Swansea

1921 caption.—Christopher Columbus. "*I ascribe my failure, Gentlemen, to the inclemency of the weather, for I assure you I have hitherto been invariably successful with this trick.*"

"I think we've been stood up."

S. H. Cohen of Manchester

1921 caption.—Sympathetic Father (to son returning to school). "*I know the feeling, old man. I used to feel just the same when my leave was up and I had to go back to France.*"
Son. "*Yes, but then you had a revolver.*"

"What's she like on cornering?"

P. G. Haywood of Leeds

1937 caption.—*"As you see, Bellamy, I haven't lost my passion for driving four-in-hand."*

"Never mind, Guv'nor. There's lots of other escaped convicts on the moor."

J. Lynch of Thornton Heath, Surrey

1921 caption.—"A HEATHER MIXTURE, CONSISTING OF ONE WASP (ANGRY), DITTO COLONEL (MORE SO), DITTO GILLIE (SAIR AFRAID), DITTO HOST (PEPPERED) AND SEVERAL GROUSE (UNHURT)."

Joint winners:

"*I think your father's put the two-way mirror in backwards.*"

J. C. Jones of Ormskirk.

"*But Dorian, we can't live on your student's grant
for the rest of our lives.*"

E. B. Parkinson of Worksop.

1872 caption.—Inductive flattery. "That is a portrait of dear papa, before he wore a beard and moustache, you know."
"Indeed, how very lovely your mamma must have been."

"*And I further declare the said Caractacus elected as
member for the above mentioned constituency.*"

A. Yelloly of Leamington Spa.

1927 caption.—THE PROMOTION OF EDUCATION IN EARLY TIMES. The Lord Eustace Percy of those days presents a flint medal to the discoverer of the fact that two and two make four.

"*. . . In a little number entitled, 'Lenin on a Lamp-post'.*"

J. Cheetham of Hertford.

1946 caption.—In Front of the Curtain: "*Please keep your seats—there's no danger.*"

"*Have you anything for flatulence?*"

K. Lee of Berkhamsted, Herts.

1915 caption.—A customer objects to a few exclusive charges in her grocer's bill.

JOINT WINNERS: "*I thought the Liberal Party Conference was at Llandudno?*"

S. Walker of Derby.

AND: "*I believe they've been chosen for a trial with Manchester United fans.*"

C. Waine of Blackburn.

1871 caption.—A GENERAL SALUTE. *Captain Dyngwell, 1st R.V. (sotto voce).* "Now, what the Dooce can these Sympson Gals mean by Looking in that ridiculous Manner?"

"*Oh Lord, it's another petition from the trawlermen.*"

N. Stock of Keyworth, Notts.

1928 caption.—ENTERTAINMENTS AT WHICH WE HAVE NEVER ASSISTED: Opening of the Smoked Fish Season: Bloater Banquet at Yarmouth.

*" You mustn't miss this! The last lot walked 400 miles,
stuck a pole in the ground and then went back again."*

N. Craig of London E11.

1930 caption.—THE ADVANCE OF CIVILIZATION. It is probable that in the near
future pleasure trips to the Arctic Regions will become popular. The Old Walrus.
"Come on, boys! Buns!"

*"I don't see my name among the obituaries, so I'll go to the
Club this afternoon."*

A. Temple Cole of Sevenoaks, Kent

1886 caption.—LEGISLATION. Alderman Gustle, M.P. (Reading the Paper at his
mid-day snack. *"Oh, I dessay! Go down to the 'Ouse at Two o'Clock, indeed! Why, it
wouldn't give me no time for Luncheon! Oh, I shall Vote against that!"*

"Where's the Manchester United match, sonny?"
J. Catanach of London SW19.

1925 caption.—Excited Knight-Errant. "*Boy! Run quickly and bring an armourer! There is a deed of daring to do here and some of my bolts have got rusted in.*"

"Which camera am I on? Having so many newsreaders is getting damn' confusing."
S. Dexter of Horley, Surrey.

1883 caption.—HISTORY OF A FAMILY PORTRAIT. Grigsby. "*By the way, that's a new Picture, Sir Pompey—the Knight in Armour, I mean!*" Sir Pompey Bedell. "*Er—yes. It came to me in rather a curious way—er—too long to relate at present. It's an Ancestor of mine—a Bedell of Richard the Third's period!*" Grigsby (who made an all but successful offer of three-seventeen-six for said Picture, last week, to old Moss Isaacs, in Wardour Street). "*By Jove, he was precious near being an Ancestor of Mine too!*" (Proceeds to explain, but is interrupted by Sir P.'s proposing to join the Ladies.)

JOINT WINNERS: *"Only one 'N' in Constable, sir."*

D. D. McGready of Reading.

AND: *"I'm calling it 'The Inside of a Brolly'."*

L. Rowley of Leeds.

1871 caption.—"THE FINISHING TOUCH!" *Farmer (who had been most Obliging, and taken great Interest in the Picture).* "Good Morn'n', Sir! But—*(aghast)*—I say, what are you a doin' of, Mister?! P'intin' all them beastly Poppies in my Corn!— 'A bit o' Colour?' What 'ould my Landlord say, d'you Think?— and after I'd put off my Cuttin' cause you hadn't finished, to oblige yer, I didn't Think you'd a Done it! You don't Come a Pintin' on my Land and more!" (Exit, in great dudgeon.)

"Watch out! It's a radar trap!"

D. Bates of Beckenham, Kent.

1881 caption—NORTH LONDONERS. Preparing for the Severities of the Coming Winter. (*After Du Chaillu.*)

"But we were just coming to borrow some sugar from you!"

M. Shotton of Cambridge.

1925 caption.—THINGS THEY DO MORE PICTURESQUELY ABROAD. Students of the University pass each other in the streets of Salzburg.

JOINT WINNERS: *"If we're caught, I'm going to have something to say to the Escape Committee about this!"*

D. Board of London SW10.

AND: *"Personally, I think Scotland's not a good place to attempt a coup from."*

I. Heath of Southsea, Hants.

1885 caption.—THE GOLF-STREAM. Flows along the Eastern Coast of Scotland during the Summer and Autumn. (Vide *Report of British Association—Section V.*)

JOINT WINNERS: *"Make that **one** cup of tea and an iced bun."*

S. Davenport of London NW3.

AND: *"Try pulling his head!"*

J. Lester of Kinoulton, Notts.

1925 caption.—Stalker (in hoarse whisper to sportsman who has been "told about it" at least twenty times). *"Keep y'r heid doon."*

"Scotland Yard? I wish to report a stolen telephone."

D. Young of Perth.

1896 caption.—"AFTER YOU!"

"Well, she must have been going at one hell of a pace when she hit the beach"

D. Hodgetts of Newcastle-upon-Tyne

1937 caption.—"CAN YOU TELL ME WHAT THAT IS?" "THAT, SIR, IS THE NEW RAILWAY TUNNEL AIR-SHAFT." "DEAR ME! HOW EXTREMELY ANNOYING FOR THE RESIDENTS." "LOR, SIR, THAT WAS THERE LONG BEFORE THE RESIDENTS."

"I still say Diogenes was offside."

G. M. Gittins of Hale Barns, Cheshire

1928 caption—DRAMATIST (ABOUT 300 BC) WHILE ON A VISIT TO HIS OLD FRIEND, EUCLID, GETS AN INSPIRATION FOR A NEW COMEDY.

"What do you mean, I haven't won this week's Caption Competition?"

J. von Achten of Hadfield, Cheshire

1921 caption.—*Seaside House Agent (to applicant for furnished house): "You don't mean to say you've got children?"*

"I prefer the pocket sun-dial—it doesn't singe the falcon."

P. Fitton of Rochdale

1933 caption—MAGNIFICENT FAILURES IN HISTORY. King Alfred tries to invent a wristwatch.

*"I still say we should invite them round and play
the game sensibly."*

D. M. Simpson of Belfast.

1878 caption.—LAWN-TENNIS UNDER DIFFICULTIES.—"PLAY!" If Space is
limited, there is no reason why one shouldn't Play with one's next-door Neighbours,
over the Garden Wall. (One needn't Visit them, you know!)

*"Come, come, ladies—after checking the mirror the signal is
the right arm fully outstretched . . ."*

B. Marshall of Derby.

1914 caption.—THIS IS NOT A CLOAK-ROOM BUT THE LOUNGE OF A FASHIONABLE LONDON
HOTEL.

"Frankly, Mr Ronay, I'm surprised you don't get indigestion more frequently."

G. W. Jones of Cowbridge, Glams.

1878 caption.—"CATCHING AT A STRAW." *Curate (visiting a poor Cabman down with Bronchitis).* "Have you been in the Habit of going to Church?" *Poor Cabby (faintly).* "Can't say I hev, Sir"—*(eagerly)*—"I've druv a good many Parties there, Sir!"

"Oh no—not a bang gang!"

A. Hancox of Saintbridge, Glos.

1914 caption.—MR PUNCH'S GALLERY OF BRAVE DEEDS. No 1. The hero who took out a party of ladies ferreting.

"More repeats! There's never anything new on the Tapestry."
C. Kennedy of Worcester Park, Surrey

"OK, so you're a three-pin plug—now where's the electric socket?"

G. Aver of Truro.

"The provisional D.I.Y. have claimed responsibility."
R. Fayle of Nottingham

1931 caption—ULTRA-MODERN NIECE. "SO SWEET OF YOU TO LOOK ME UP, UNCLE! TAKE THE EASY-CHAIR."

"Have you seen anyone run past carrying four pairs of braces?"
S. Baker of Rumtree, Notts.

1896 caption—*CLERK OF BOOKING OFFICE.* "THERE IS *NO* FIRST CLASS BY THIS TRAIN, SIR."
'ARRY. "THEN WOT ARE *WE* GOING TER DO, BILL?"

"Four singles to Waterloo, please."

D. B. Whitmore of Penicuik, Midlothian.

1914 caption.—GETTING USED TO THE "SMILING EXPRESSION". Our suggestion for a system of advanced physical training for Prussian officers before taking up commands in the Alsatian district, where the populace is said to be addicted to humour.

"We go supersonic after Potters Bar."

R. A. Watson, of Scarborough.

1914 caption.—AN ALTRUIST MALGRÉ LUI

"So that's forty milk and sugar. . . . "

M. Procter of London W9

"Exactly two hours, ten minutes since we gave up smoking."

J. Benton, of Birmingham.

" You can spot the party from Weightwatchers the minute the house lights go down."

M. J. Matthews of Birmingham.

1914 caption.—A THEATRICAL REVIVAL. AT THE LITTLE THEATRE MR BERTRAM FORSYTH PROPOSES TO REPRODUCE SCENES FROM PLAYS AS THEY WERE PRESENTED 100 OR 150 YEARS AGO. HE WILL TRY, WE ARE TOLD, TO RESTORE THE OLD-TIME ATMOSPHERE. AN ORANGE-WOMAN WILL NIGHTLY CARRY HER BASKET THROUGH THE THEATRE.

"Get moving in the back there, Holmes, they've just let the bull in."

C. Loach of Leicester.

1929 caption.—Muffled Voice from inside. *"Do be careful where you're sitting, darling: you'll have the tent down."*

*"Oh, somebody please help—is there a hair stylist
in the house?"*

M. J. Foy of Southend-on-Sea.

1914 caption.—THE SEX'S PROGRESS. From "Women at Prize-Fights" to "Women in the Ring" should be an easy step in the upward movement.

*"Stick to medicine, Dr Jekyll, Hollywood's
full of tap-dancers."*

T. P. Eckersley of Oldham, Lancs.

1858 caption.—AN INTERESTING QUESTION. Young Swell (who has just received promise of a commission in a Highland Regiment) *"Now, girls, will the kilt suit my calves?"* Sisters (tittering) *"Really, dear, you are too absurd."*

*"I say, Attenborough, this could be
the longest worm on record."*

M. White of Croydon, Surrey.

1915 caption.—*Patriotic villager (discussing ages).* "If this war 'ad only started thirty
years ago, Sir, I could just 'a squeezed into the Army."

*"You're devilish slow, Lucan—are you sure you're used to
this sort of work?"*

J. Butler of Thornton Heath, Surrey

1877 caption—MONEY "TIGHT." *BRITISH SUBALTERN.* "BY-THE-BY, SMITH, CAN
YOU LEND ME THAT SOVEREIGN I GAVE YOU THIS MORNING FOR A
CHRISTMAS-BOX?!"

"I think this rules out a coalition."

B. Millward of Newquay, Cornwall.

1872 caption.—HOME RULE. (A wild drame of the future, bedad!) (Committee of the Whole House.)

"Good morning, madam, I'd like to demonstrate our new cordless vacuum-cleaner."

G. Duffy of Newburyport, Massachusetts.

1936 caption.—"But he's only a baby, dear, and he seemed to be lost behind the gas-works, so what else could I do?"

"Well—that's the VAT Inspector's visit over for the year."
J. Behr of Yattenden, Berks.

1915 caption.—GRIT. The morning after the Zeppelin raid in our village.

"I do wish they would scrape up the chewing gum before the dance."

R. Miller of Stoke-on-Trent

1909 caption.—THE POETRY OF MOTION. "THE BORSTON."

"Well, I still think it's a cowardly way to kill a turkey."

B. M. Huxley of Hornchurch, Essex.

1911 caption.—For Country House-Parties. "Spot the Jabber." The player under the rug must guess who holds the fork.

"Sorry, Nurse, the betting is closed once we've actually poisoned the cup for the day."

B. Bailey of London.

1936 caption.—"Why are there no saucers with those cups?" "The tea ain't 'ot enough for saucers, Sister."

"Happens every year, the moment Magnus Pyke arrives."

A. Cavey of Carshalton

1936 caption.—FANCY PICTURE OF A MEETING OF THE "ASSOCIATION OF FIXED AND FLEXIBLE TRUST" MANAGERS.

"Waiter—I think we'll have the sheeps' eyeballs after all."

I. Dagger of Oldham, Lancs.

1868 caption.—MODEST APPEAL. Lady (to big drum). "*Pray, my good Man, don't make that horrid Noise! I can't hear myself Speak!*"

"It's no good, Miss—I don't know who painted him on but I can't shift it."

R. Falconer of Cardiff

1913 caption.—A VENDETTA? NOT AT ALL. GIUSEPPE AND LUIGI ARE ENGAGED IN THE MORNING CONFLICT WITH THEIR MASTER'S WINDOW.

"I've operated four times now, but I still can't find a place for this bit."

N. Fell of Aberdeen.

1886 caption.—THE POWER OF THE IMAGINATION. Street Arab (to Doctor, who has just been taking his temperature). *"Ah, Sir! That done me a lot o' Good, Sir!"*

*"I only said I was **thinking** of opening an account."*

A. J. Mitchell of Woldingham.

1914 caption.—[Circular from head office of a London bank to its branches: "Suggested that the Cashier should drop his cash-scoop as a warning to the remainder of the staff that a forged cheque is being presented and that they are to detain the presenter."] The cashier at our Goldstead branch has the misfortune to drop his scoop accidentally when cashing a cheque for the worthy mayor of our select suburb.

"No, these are Constables—the Sargents are next door."

M. Maltman of Glasgow.

1914 caption.—THE MILITANT SCANDAL. II.—The skied artist comes into his own.

JOINT WINNERS: "*Stone me—better mark that one up as High Tar Content!*"

B. Eastwell of Carshalton Beeches, Surrey.

AND: "*Well, it woke you up all right—but where's the tea?*"

M. Jones of Portsmouth.

1856 caption.—TAKE CARE THAT YOU MANAGE THE APPARATUS PROPERLY.

"*No further, mate, this is the pâté de foie gras picket line.*"

M. Clarke of Chigwell, Essex.

1928 caption.—APPRECIATION. Derelict Actor of Villains' parts. "*Ha! They hiss me!*"

"The C.O. likes his kebabs served with a bit of style."
D. Tidy of New Romney, Kent

1867 caption—BROWN HAS HEARD "ON GOOD AUTHORITY" THAT THE BRITISH YEOMANRY CAVALRY WILL BE REVIEWED BY THE SULTAN, AND RESOLVES IT SHAN'T BE HIS FAULT IF THEY DON'T MAKE A SENSATION; SO HE "TIPS" AN INSTRUCTOR TO PRIVATELY PUT HIM THROUGH THE MOUNTED EXERCISE!

"It was a bit of a struggle but, as you can see, the woodworm finally surrendered."
W. Smith of Cambridge

1920 caption—LANDLADY (SHOWING APARTMENTS IN THE VICINITY OF FAMOUS LINKS). "OH, YOU'LL BE QUITE COMFORTABLE HERE, SIR; YOU SEE, WE'RE USED TO GOLFERS."

"And what does Miss Rice-Davies say about the rest of us?"

A. Pantin of Harrogate

"I was certain I'd left my middle two fingers down here."

B. Henman of Guildford

"I agree it's a weak show but myxomatosis killed the business."

I. Brown of Cambridge

1936 caption.—"NO, NO, YOUR MAJESTY, NOT THE ROPE TRICK, PLEASE DON'T ASK ME: I'M SICK OF HEARING THE WORD MESMERISM."

"I see that the Gardeners' Question Time team claim responsibility."

M. Birt of Cheltenham

1869 caption—A RURAL STUDY. Burlesque-writer forcing puns.

"We keeps using dem birth control pills, Father, but all we get is radishes."

F. X. Sullivan of Liverpool

1908 caption *MRS. GILES (ANXIOUSLY ASKING AFTER RECTOR'S HEALTH).* "WELL, SIR, I BE GLAD YOU SAYS YOU' BE WELL, BUT THERE—YOU BE ONE OT THESE 'BAD DOERS,' AS I CALLS 'EM. GIE 'EM THE BEST O' VITTELS, AND IT DON'T DO 'EM NO GOOD. *THERE BE PIGS LIKE THAT!"*

"Oh, the engine-tuners are back—it's the body-fitters now."

P. Fitton of Cambridge.

1885 caption.—" *'Old yer Oss, Sir?"*

*"I've come about that magician's outfit
I purchased for my grandson."*

B. Stott of Blackpool.

*"I suddenly remembered I lent him my watch
just before the sad day."*

P. Blathwayt of Bath.

JOINT WINNERS: "*I take it this means Mr Ronay was not impressed.*"

L. A. Davies of Huntingdon.

AND: "*First bionic mouse or not, it's got to go.*"

P. J. Wiehl of Bradford.

1915 caption.—A boarder points out to his landlady that his breakfast egg is not altogether to his taste.

"*You clout her on the head with the brick and I'll grab her handbag.*"

B. Lambert of Rugby.

1871 caption.—"THOUGHT IS FREE." The Tempest. *Miss Minerva Bristlington* (*fiercely*). "'*Honour* and *obey*,' indeed! Ha! Ha! I should just like to see a man ask *me* to '*honour* and *obey*' him!" ("*I've no doubt that you'd like to see him* very much indeed!" *thought the two Miss Marigolds—but they didn't say so.*)

"So much for solar energy—this one isn't nearly done."

C. Thomson of Glasgow

1910 caption—PATROL LEADER (WAKING UP OLD GENTLEMAN). "FORGIVE MY TROUBLING YOU. SIR. BUT WOULD YOU MIND SLEEPING EAST AND WEST AS WE EXPECT THE ENEMY FROM THE NORTH AND ARE BADLY IN WANT OF COVER ?"

"I can't be sure, Inspector—perhaps if I could see them in soiled raincoats. . ."

A. Heal of Swafield, Norfolk.

1915 caption.—Lady X is interviewed as to her opinions on thrift in war-time.

"Sometimes I wish we'd been joined at the hip."

T. Hopkins of Luton

1936 caption. —"GOOD SHOW?" "FOUL." "COCKTAILS?" "WIZARD."

"And what about the premiums for the same policy with profits?"

N. Craig of London E.11

1927 caption.—Pamela. *"How's your wife, Peter?"* Peter. *"She died last Tuesday."* Pamela. *"Are you sorry?"* Peter. *"Sorry? I liked the woman."*

"*That's the trouble with the twenties—everyone has the Twenties' Look.*"

T. Hopkins of Luton.

1930 caption.—"*My dear husband dislikes being thought stout, so I always make a point of **not** thinking him stout.*"

"*These cash and carry oil rigs will never catch on.*"

J. Sharpe of Redbridge, Essex.

1902 caption.—("*It has been decided at a meeting of prominent yachtsmen, to found a Marine Motor Association.*" Vide "Daily Telegraph.") Our Anticipatory Artist has a vision of an endless vista of pleasant Marine-Motor Week-ends.

*"If this one doesn't work, sir, I move we elect a new
Escape Officer."*

G. Jones of Cowbridge, Glamorgan.

1902 caption.—OXFORD OF THE FUTURE. Rhodes Scholar U.S.A. (to old-fashioned Lecturer, who has rather overstepped the time limit). *"Say, Professor, guess you had better quit. I've gotten an appointment down town!"* (Collapse of O.F.L. in a dead (language) faint.)

"God—these store detectives are very persistent."

C. Waine of Blackburn.

1878 caption.—HAPPY THOUGHT. The good old Game of "Hare and Hounds," or "Paper-Chase," is still played in the Northern Suburbs of London during the Winter. Why should not Young Ladies be the Hares?

"Quite cold and greasy enough, Mrs Brown, but could you cope with running the business side of a motorway service station?"

E. O. Parrott of London W8

1937 caption.—*VISITOR.* "SEE—EVEN THE LITTLE PIG KNOWS ME."
FARMER'S WIFE. "'TAIN'T YOU 'E KNOWS, LADY—'TIS 'IS LITTLE BOWL."

"As Chairman of this Enquiry into the effects of cannabis smoking . . ."

R. Pratt of Sutton Coldfield.

1892 caption.—STUDIES IN ANIMAL LIFE. THE GOORMONG. (Epicuri de Grege Porcus. British Isles.) Mr. Huggins. *"What a 'eavenly Dinner it was!"* Mr. Buggins. *"B'lieve yer! Mykes yer wish yer was born 'Oller!"*

"Then again, I think everyone gets depressed at this time of year."

T. Eckersley of Oldham

1928 caption—"SHIPWRECKED MARINER (AS IT BEGINS TO SNOW), "LET ME SEE—WASN'T IT ARNOLD BENNETT WHO SAID, 'NOTHING IS TOO GOOD TO BE TRUE'?"

"Look, dear! Your obituary has come out a day early."

D. Young of Perth.

1925 caption.—Wife of victim of an accident. "*Look, Alfred. Isn't it jolly? You've got your photo in the paper!*"

*"You've been picketing an artist's impression—
the factory is over there."*

C. Waine of Blackburn

1937 caption.—**MODEL EMPLOYER.** "NOW, BATES, I WANT YOU TO ASCERTAIN THE GENERAL OPINION OF THE FACTORY—GERANIUMS OR ANTIRRHINUMS."

*"It's all on who can keep his hand there the longest before
they get to the bar."*

J. Rule of London NW7

1933 caption—**LONDON LIFE.** A PROFESSOR OF DEPORTMENT GIVING A LESSON TO MEMBERS OF PARLIAMENT IN THE ART OF "CROSSING THE FLOOR OF THE HOUSE."

"Always pays to read the small print in a Dr Who script."

C. Thompson of Glasgow

1931 caption—THE HIGHER HORTICULTURE. Convalescent cactus being taken out for an airing in Kew Gardens.

"I wish they'd knock a few of us off this job—I think he suspects something."

R. Watson of Malvern, Worcs.

1882 caption.—THE MORNING PAPERS. Sketch from our Window, Ten a.m., at Sludgeborough Ness.

"Yes, since we left Marlboro country I'm down to ninety a day."

P. Fitton of Rochdale

1869 caption—"ANY OBJECTION TO A CIGAR, SIR?" "PERSONALLY, SIR, NONE WHATEVER; BUT I HAPPEN TO BE A DIRECTOR, WHY——" "HAW! BY JOVE! THEN WHY THE DOOCE DON'T YOU MAKE THEM KEEP BETTER TIME?"

"OK—the dove's returned. So what?"
J. McCarthy of Lancaster.

1925 caption—BILLIARDS AT THE ZOO. *THE BEAR.* "LET'S SEE, OLD MAN, DID YOU SAY YOU WERE SPOT?" *THE LEOPARD.* "DON'T BE SILLY!"

"Sorry, Missus, children bought at sale time aren't exchangeable."

B. Henman of Guildford

"Can you hide these political prisoners from Iran?"

L. Mantel of Cambridge.

"Sight screens have certainly changed since Schweppes started sponsoring test cricket."
B. Edwards of Wrexham

1925 caption—DARE WE HOPE THAT OUR R.A.'s, AFTER THEIR ADMIRABLE WORK IN IMPROVING THE STANDARD OF OUR RAILWAY POSTERS, WILL NOW TURN THEIR ATTENTION TO OUR ELECTRIC SIGNS.

"Looks like Gulliver's got a boiled egg for breakfast again."
P. Mansell of Birmingham.

1877 caption—OUR CHINAMANIACS ABOARD. MILD (BUT FIRM) DEMEANOUR OF THE PRIGSBYS, WHO COLLECT ORIENTAL BLUE, BEFORE A "VASE EN PORCELAINE DE SEVRES."

"Oh go on—please sing us the one about the manic depressive again."

L. Armstrong of Newport

"We are now over the council houses which are for sale."

M. Birt of Gloucestershire

"You can stop pumping now, Jeeves, she's about the right size."

A. George of Derbyshire

"Actually, we haven't had a public disembowelling for some time."

C. Jones of Lancashire.

"You're on the wrong track, Mr Holmes—this is the gerbil of the Baskervilles."

P. Fitton of Rochdale

1877 caption—"ALL IN THE DAY'S WORK." *Gigantic footman.* "DID YOU RING, MA'AM?" *Tender-hearted and Impulsive Lady* "YES, THOMAS. YOU SEE THIS POOR KITTEN THE CHILDREN HAVE FOUND? IT IS MOTHERLESS! GET SOME MILK, THOMAS! MEW LIKE ITS MOTHER!—AND FEED IT!"

"Quick—hand me the chewing-gum before the reactor goes critical."

P. Huett of Weymouth.

1926 caption—PLUMMER. "YES, SIR. THERE'S SOME OF 'EM STILL TORKIN' ABAHT THE DRY SUMMER WE 'AD."

"That's it, no more North Sea oil."

R. Gerlls of Ilford.

1905 caption—THE NORTH SEA COMMISSIONERS MAKE A THOROUGH INVESTIGATION OF THE DOGGER BANK. ("THE ONLY CIRCUMSTANTIAL EVIDENCE OF THE PRESENCE OF JAPANESE TORPEDO BOATS IS AT THE BOTTOM OF THE NORTH SEA, WHITHER THE COMMISSION OF INQUIRY CANNOT TRANSFER ITS INVESTIGATIONS WITHOUT SERIOUS INCONVENIENCE."— *THE TIMES, JAN 10.*)

"Guy's Hospital Emergency Thyroid Gland Unit—and step on it!"

L. File of Ramsgate

1930 caption—A LIFT TO THE STATION. WHAT OUR GOOD SAMARITANS HAVE TO PUT UP WITH.

"I don't know about you, Alf, but I always thought transvestism would be more exciting than this."
P. Scoging of West Molesey, Surrey.

1930 caption—*FIRST YOUNG LADY.* "I SAY, THERE'S A TOPPING ARTICLE HERE ON THE IMPORTANCE OF POISE." *SECOND YOUNG LADY* "I KNOW; I'VE READ IT."

"Irish AA at your service, sorr."
T. Blunt of Derby

1901 caption—MOTORIST (A NOVICE) HAS BEEN GIVING CHAIRMAN OF LOCAL URBAN COUNCIL A PRACTICAL DEMONSTRATION OF THE EASE WITH WHICH A MOTOR-CAR CAN BE CONTROLLED WHEN TRAVELLING AT HIGH SPEED.

"Saddle up, you two—the Light Brigade needs a round six hundred for the poem to scan."

P. C. Fitton of Rochdale

1900 caption—*SQUADRON OFFICER.* 'YOU TOLD ME YOU HAD ANOTHER HORSE AT HOME, AND I GAVE YOU A DAY'S LEAVE TO FETCH HIM." *TROOPER T.* "AY, CAP'EN AND SO I DID. *SQUADRON OFFICER.* "WELL, WHY ISN'T IT HERE NOW?" *TROOPER T.* "AY, CAP'EN, BUT I COULDN'T CATCH HIM. HE'S BEEN ON T'GRASS SO LONG, THAT HE BE FAIR WILD, HE DEW!'

"My God! It's coming back!"

F. Line of Birmingham

1939 caption—"YOU TIRESOME CHILD! *I TOLD* YOU NOT TO PRESS THAT BUTTON!"

"Don't worry, ladies, I'll serve him these paternity notices if it's the last thing I do!"
P. Foulds of London SE2

1900 caption—TATTERSALL'S OF THE FUTURE. AUCTIONEER (QUOTING FROM CATALOGUE). "LOT FIFTEEN. A PERFECT HACK. BEEN CARRYING A LADY PEDAL AT BATTERSEA DURING THE SEASON. SOUND IN WIND AND SPOKES. OWNER GONE ABROAD. NOW, MAY I SAY THIRTY?"

"You'll find a term at Harrods has changed your son a lot."
D. Jones of Cardiff.

1925 caption—"I WANT A LITTLE MASCOT FOR MY CAR. DO YOU KEEP SUCH THINGS?" "YES, MADAM. MR SAMPSON—FORWARD!"

"It's the first time we've tried computer dating."
H. Kirk of Hull.

"I'm afraid you've come to the wrong place, mate—the Surrealist landscape is about two miles over there."

K. Green of Cambridge

". . . and a Pheasant Tandoori for table 14!"

R. Taylor of Sevenoaks

1900 caption—EXTRACT FROM THE "MUDDLETON MERCURY":—"PROMINENT AMONG THE FOLLOWERS OF THE HOLDUM HARRIERS, ON MONDAY LAST, WE NOTICED THE MAHARAJAH OF BUNDAPORE, WHO ATTRACTED A GOOD DEAL OF ATTENTION."

"I always find lots of loose change after Uncle Gerald has been to see you."

D. R. Davies of Worcester.

1877 caption—"TROP DE ZELE!" *(TOMMY, A CONSCIENTIOUS BOY, HAS BEEN TOLD THAT HE MUST REMAIN PERFECTLY STILL, AS HIS MAMMA WANTS TO TAKE A NAP.)* TOMMY *(IN THE MIDDLE OF THE NAP),* "MAMMA! MAMMA! WHAT SHALL I DO? I WANT TO COUGH!"

"What sort of armed escort do you expect for 50 p?"

R.J. Andrews of Hereford

1901 caption: Ruling the road. "Now, my good woman, if you can't pull them out of the way, you must let them go. We have to catch a train!" "Yus. And who d'you s'pose 'ud ketch my pigs."

"I see they're taking a tougher approach to selling War Cry."

R. Falconer of Cardiff.

1930 caption—THE SPREAD OF ART CULTURE. REGRETTABLE AFFAIR AT AN EAST END DARTS CLUB, CAUSED BY A DIFFERENCE OF OPINION ON THE RELATIVE MERITS OF THE UMBRIAN AND VENETIAN SCHOOLS OF PAINTING.

"But, Your Majesty, you're the one person relied on to stay for the National Anthem."

C. Thomson of Glasgow.

1905 caption—SWEEPING ASSERTION. "THE OTHER NIGHT, AT THE NOVELTY THEATRE, MRS VERE-JONES WAS GOWNED SIMPLY IN A CLINGING BLACK VELVET, WITH A CLOAK OF SAME HANDSOMELY TRIMMED WITH ERMINE." *EXTRACT FROM SOCIETY JOURNAL.*

"I hear he got his pacemaker on the NHS."

G. Easter of Wembley.

1905 caption—THE PORTABLE GRAMOPHONE. DANCE WHERE AND WHEN YOU LIKE. CHOOSE YOUR OWN TIME AND TUNE. NO COUNTRY HOUSE SHOULD BE WITHOUT IT.

"It's based on the animated picture version of the light operetta composed for the phonograph from the original magic lantern production."

J. Rule of London NW7.

"And don't come back until you're wearing a tie!"

A. Bazeley of London W1

". . . 98, 99, 100—coming, ready or not!"
K. Cowdall of Liverpool

1877 caption—A SENSITIVE PLANT. (HERR PUMPERNICKEL, HAVING JUST PLAYED A COMPOSITION OF HIS OWN, BURSTS INTO TEARS.) *CHORUS OF FRIENDS:* "OH, WHAT IS THE MATTER! WHAT CAN WE DO FOR YOU?" *HERR PUMPERNICKEL:* "ACH! NOSSING! NOSSING! BOT VEN I HEAR REALLY *COOT* MUSIC, ZEN MUST I ALWAYS VEEP!"

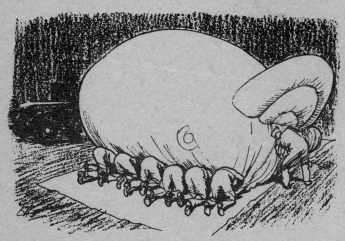

JOINT WINNERS: *"Hold it! I've found the puncture."*
K. Greaves of The Wirral

AND: *"We seem to have landed in Muslim country, sir."*
A. Powling of Plymouth

1939 caption—"TUCKING UP THE KIDBROOKE BABY" TECHNICAL DISPLAY (BALLOON-BARRAGE) BY THE R.A.F.

"Of course, in the old days we didn't have stewardesses."

A. Mitchell of Woldingham, Surrey.

1925 caption.—THE PILLION GIRL: NEXT STEP.

"But sir, The East India Co brochure made no mention of Virginity Tests!"

H. Morris of Cambridge

1896 caption—A DECLARATION INDEED! "AVEZ-VOUS QUELQUECHOSE A DECLARER, MADAME?" "OH, WEE! JE DECLAR QUE NOOS AVONG PAIRDEW TOO NO BAGGARGE!"

"If, however, the fly is settling from the right . . ."
E. Makin of Liverpool

1931 caption—ENTERTAINMENTS AT WHICH WE HAVE NEVER ASSISTED. "STRIKING THE HAPPY MEDIUM" AT THE SOCIETY FOR PSYCHICAL RESEARCH.

"Why not show them how you snatch the cloth off without disturbing the settings?"
E. Hampson of Southampton

1882 caption—*MISS LUCY.* "HERE'S WHERE YOU AND I ARE TO SIT, MAJOR!" *THE MAJOR.* "BY JOVE!—A—RATHER A WARM PLACE!" *MISS LUCY.* "WHAT—YOU A MAJOR AND CAN'T STAND FIRE!" *THE MAJOR.* "NOT *AT MY BACK,* YOU KNOW, MISS LUCY!"

*"Nearly everyone who jumps from the fourteenth floor
seems to land on that branch."*

A. Pantin of Harrogate

"For the same money Picasso gives you two heads."

G. Hughes of Cardiff